Trade Show Guide to Success

By Bert Kenyon

Table of Contents

Chapter 1 - Why this will Help! - *Page 3*

Chapter 2 - General Challenges - *Page 7*

Chapter 3 - Potential Customer - *Page 9*

Chapter 4 - The Right Show - *Page 10*

Chapter 5 - What is your Goal - *Page 13*

Chapter 6 - Budget, Cost - *Page 20*

Chapter 7- Image Concept - *Page 23*

Chapter 8 - Design your Booth - *Page 25*

Chapter 9 - Destination Booths - *Page 35*

Chapter 10 - Booth Staff - *Page 46*

Chapter 11 - Working the Booth - *Page 49*

Chapter 12 - Post Market - *Page 58*

Chapter 13 - Summary - *Page 60*

Contact Information - *Page 61*

Trade Show Guide to Success

Chapter 1 - Why this guide will help you!

Want to make your trade show program more successful? Let's do that!

Whether you're starting to plan your first trade show, you've been doing it for a while and still getting poor results or you're a professional at it and believe you are the best, this guide should be helpful to everyone.

Most channels of businesses or professions have a trade organization and most of those have some type of Trade Show or Market. As a matter of fact, there are over 5000 different trade shows a year in America alone. They can differ from small, intimate gatherings to huge shows with thousands of exhibitors spanning a couple of weeks. Many are local or regional, some National and a few are International, but all of them are relatively expensive, proportionate to the size of the industry. Because of that, it's important that you accomplish what is necessary for that effort and investment.

Let me interject here and say, going forward in this guide, all Trade Shows and Markets will just be called Shows.

Differences in Show Experience:

What I have found in over 57 years of being involved in shows, is that almost all new exhibitors don't understand the basics of what is necessary, therefore are wasting their money.

Those that may have been doing it a while, understand the basic's but are frustrated because of the poor return on their show investment. That can be either the lack of orders written or not increasing their business as hoped. Either way, the pressure is on to justify the ongoing cost.

Then there are those folks that are more difficult to help because they either have been doing trade shows for a long time or because they are responsible for the company's program, they don't want to accept the fact that they could use some advice.

Though it's understandable that they might want to protect their image, it's also short-sighted. Why not be open minded and possibly improve your company's performance by seeing what others are doing. I've never seen a trade show program that couldn't use some improvement. Very few are maximizing their ROI.

I'm always astounded at how much money is wasted on ill-prepared and improperly executed trade show programs. I wouldn't even try to guess how many hours of my life I have spent on one side of the aisle or the other, but I am a very hands-on, observant person and guilty of being a perfectionist.

Given the extreme difference in businesses and their goals, some of the strategies or suggestions may not be appropriate for you specifically, but some of the concepts should. I was told a long time ago, if you are a creative type personality, *"Teach me one principal, and I will extrapolate that into 1000 applications."*

If you only improve your show performance or ROI by 10%, this read will have been worthwhile. Hopefully, some readers will be motivated to completely revisit the show program. So please put your ego aside, understand the concepts, apply what is appropriate for your industry and start making an increased profit off what is currently a huge, contentious expense.

Chapter 2 - General Challenges

Very few vendors get excited about trade shows and most consider them a painful necessity. That's really a shame because if done correctly, they can be a very profitable and rewarding investment. Also, proper planning can eliminate most of the challenges. I have told many vendors who gripe about so many shows, that if you do it right, and each show/market is profitable, does it really matter how many there are. Only if you put a minimum effort into them, are they an unrewarding expense

There is an old Trade Show saying, *"You get out of them, what you put into them."* I've been able to make almost every market, for almost every vendor who pays attention, a profitable investment.

Wasted money, Worthless Booths:

During the last three months of 2018, I attended my final trade shows as a rep and said goodbye to many dealers who have become good friends over the years. When they asked what I was going to be doing next and I explained my new direction of helping manufacturers with their trade show programs, they all agreed it was certainly needed.

Upon querying them about those comments, unanimously they said that the vast majority of the booths were either a total waste of the vendors' money or were far from maximizing their ROI. The booths either didn't have a person in the booth, that person was too busy speaking to someone else, there were no apparent promotions, or the exhibitor/rep did not have enough knowledge/interest to help them make decisions or solve their problems.

Several said something like *"Why do vendors spend so much money for no return."* Well, let's see if we can change that!

Chapter 3 – Your Potential Customer

Some first questions are:
- What Industry are you in and why are you considering trade shows?
- What is it that you are trying to accomplish?
- Does your target customer need to be sold on your category or your product/service or are they already familiar with it and your trying to get them to buy from you rather than a competitor?

These are important points to understand fully because they set the foundation as to how you approach your trade show program.

Chapter 4 – Which Show is Right for you?

Obviously, your industry has tradeshows or you wouldn't be planning on exhibiting in them. What type of show are they? Some businesses simply have shows to trade ideas or just build relationships. Others are there to introduce new ideas, but the vast majority is to promote those businesses or sell products. If the shows are the latter, then is it B2B or to the end consumers?

Driving down even further, here are some of the reasons for exploring the possibilities of getting involved in trade shows:
- Introducing a new company into a certain channel of business or to the public in general.
- Introducing a new product or program into an existing channel or distributor.
- To build brand recognition, whether you're a new or existing brand.
- Certainly, the most prominent reason, to sell a product, whether at the show or post-show.

Once you have decided that you should start investing in shows, which shows are appropriate?

If you haven't exhibited in any shows or a particular show yet, there are many things to consider:

What different shows are available, and which are most appropriate for your specific purpose? Make sure you totally understand the function of each show, who attends and how well is it attended. Many shows have deceiving names and the show may not serve your goals.

Often a channel of business may have several shows, but for specific reasons.
A friend had a new idea for handling eggs, so he went to a Chicken show. After the second day of no one showing any interest in his product at all, he asked a fellow vendor what he was doing wrong. He was told he was at the wrong show, *"This is a Chicken show, not an Egg show"*.
Make sure the show you've picked meets your needs.

Is this a new market for you? If so, have you attended that show before and do you know how it works? Optimally it's best if you understand the exact aspects of it by attending one before.

Is it well attended and by whom? Are they really your target customer?

You don't want to attend a show without knowing in advance how the show works, what opportunities for Pre-Promoting your program are available, what level of attendees come to the show and how best to get the most return for your investment. I believe that a large percentage of first-time exhibitors waste their money by not understanding their first show. Then they are discouraged, can't justify the expense and then they are fighting an uphill battle going forward.

Chapter 5 – What is your Goal?

What are you trying to accomplish? Is it a selling show or an identity show?

If you're looking for a selling show, will you be selling direct or through a distributor. Your method of promoting will be completely different based on the target customer.

Consumer as a Target

Selling to a consumer is easier because you only need to attract them to your booth, then meet the needs/expectation of that individual target customer with your product to make the sale. Is your target customer the general population, a specific interest group or a certain generation?

Obviously, you should be fairly well versed in that focus consumer, so knowing their needs should be easy. But knowing what will gain their attention may be something else. If you don't have someone in your organization who is involved in that interest or age group, you certainly should do your research as to their interests or requirements.

It seems logical that this would happen, but we've all seen even huge companies that totally miss the market. It's like the new product committee or marketing department designs what they like or drives them without considering the real end user. At 75, I wouldn't start to presume what would motivate a Millennial.

Targeting Business to Business.

If you're selling to a B2B, especially through distribution, it is a whole different program as you have several more layers to consider:

- What are the necessary parameters that are necessary to facilitate the distributor's needs and what excites them? For them, often the backside terms, promotional funds or ability to flow through their facility is as, or more important than specifications or pricing.
- Next, what does it take for the dealers to successfully sell your product? Have you solved the problem of no extra display space? I have yet to see a retailer of any type that has extra space that they need filling. Finding a way to

fit your product into an already full store is critical.
- What type of Point of Purchase sales tools are you providing?
- How about Ad layouts or advertising allowances?
- Are you able to supply your products with the latest inventory and checkout technology?
- Is your packaging and instructions Bi or Trilingual? Today that is almost a necessity.
- Finally, have you also answered all of the questions for the end user?

The reasons for any ineffectiveness can be as varied as the type of industries. Probably the biggest reason is a lack of preplanning or preparedness.

Also, there often is the challenge of their program being coordinated by internal departments who either haven't attended many shows, haven't really worked them or are going off of input from college professors who have never worked a show and are spouting theory.

Do you have a long-term plan as to what you need to accomplish, and have you established rational steps that are quantifiable? How can you expect to be successful if you don't know where you want to be?

These goals should include short term explicit expectations based off of long-term objectives. Your trade show programs should have a step by step, definitive target for each show that can be measured and then modified. That way the next show can be even more successful, all reaching towards that end goal.

Your program should have full corporate backing because it is a waste of money to jump into a trade show initiative that doesn't have a long-term commitment. Very seldom are programs an immediate hit; fulfilling everyone's expectations. The long-term goal and expense should be well laid out and agreed to.

Any program that's being designed should have the input of all parties involved. This is all internal departments, your rep if appropriate, the distributor's buyer if appropriate and input from the dealers if possible. This should never be just the Marketing Departments thoughts alone.

I can't count the number of vendor initiatives that gave no thought as to how it will work going into a certain account or channel. The people on the street know what works and what doesn't. Just because it sounds good in a committee meeting or from some professors' viewpoint doesn't mean it works for all (or any) accounts.

Different channels have different needs and the program must work for that customer specifically. Top-down marketing just does not work. Everyone needs to be totally aware of the program's goals and timetable.

Be careful of your rep's input. Just because they call on a certain account or channel, doesn't mean they know all of the intricacies. Find out from the buyer or end customer how successful that rep is and if they know what they're doing. While many reps call on different channels, there are only a few reps that really are knowledgeable and professional.

Probably the biggest mistake vendors make is a last-minute, thrown together show program just to make deadlines, with no real long-term marketing program. Again, this should be part of a well-planned out marketing program for the year with specific goals such as introducing new products, getting more products into a store or warehouse, increasing business or even solving problems and repairing damage.

First-time exhibitors especially are seldom successful, so it's important to have a well-planned strategy and practical expectations. With the proper plans in place though, you can lay down a great foundation to your overall goal.

What ROI are you expecting?

It's also necessary to establish a serious budget that will meet those goals? I find that many exhibitors fail because they haven't been realistic about the financial commitment it will take to succeed in what they are trying to accomplish. So, they start off without a solid plan or credible budget, find it takes far longer than expected, then realize it is going to cost a lot more than they planned for. Then they quit before fruition. Money, time and opportunities are wasted because of unrealistic expectations. It would be better to have a rational budget based on long-term commitment even if it means taking smaller steps to get there in the beginning. Then you will have the funds to get to your target.

Chapter 6 – What is your Budget and Minimizing Costs

Most of the time, the booth cost is only a small portion of the cost of a show. Some, but certainly not all of the additional costs are:
- The dedicated time necessary to design and initiate a successful program.
    - This is a real cost that most vendors don't include
- The physical booth itself.
    - Whether you will build it in-house or use a Trade Show Booth provider, there are questions to answer first.
    - Can you design your booth to be easily put together, hopefully without Union Labor?
    - Will it be used over and over?
    - Can it be easily modified so that it will look different for each show with a minimum of expense?
    - Will it be easy and inexpensive to ship from show to show?
    - What will the freight cost be both ways?
    - How can you minimize the freight cost by proper planning?

- Can it be stored in the booth during the show, eliminating the wait for show personnel to deliver it after the show is over?
- Will it require Electricity to be paid for (or any other type of Utility?)
- What will the storage cost be between shows?
- Be VERY Careful to eliminate Forced Freight. Plan way ahead so that your shipment arrives towards the start of the acceptance period, not toward the end.

- The cost of Booth Personnel:
  - How many will be attending and their cost?
  - Considering all of the other costs, minimizing booth personnel is short-sighted.
  - What do their housing, travel, and food cost?
  - Will you have special shirts or uniforms?
- What will Pre-Show advertising and Post-Show follow-up cost?

- Show Promotional cost including catalogs, handouts, giveaways, etc.

Chapter 7 – Image Concept

Now that you've decided to attend a certain show or series of shows, you know who your target customer is, and you've set the budget, it's a good time to talk about the four steps to being successful in your Trade Show; that's **Attraction, Interest, Desire, and Action**.

Attraction: That old adage that says *"Perception is Everything"* absolutely applies to Trade Show Booths. I have seen many great concepts, products or start-up companies that attend a show, but look like they brought a table and few samples and then thought they would attract because they had the best idea ever. Surprise, no one had interest.

But then I've seen some of the dumbest ideas or products that had a superior, professional and interesting booth that was super successful because the booth looked super successful. You must portray the right image first time out.

Interest: What is there about your booth or presentation that makes attendees want to stop and take notice. If you blend in with the rest of the row of exhibitors, you just lost any chance of drawing them in.

Desire: When the potential buyer actually comes into your booth, are you ready with all of the reasons WHY they should have interest or buy your product? This has to be on the tip of your tongue and well-practiced.

Action: if you're able to get them into your booth, this is the time to sell. I mean really sell; if you don't know how to easily engage and sell the product, you shouldn't be in the booth. It is astounding to me how a VERY large percentage of booth personnel have no idea what the word selling means. Action: Now close the sale. Whether it's taking an order right there, securing an appointment for after the show or at least getting a commitment for them to try the product, there must be some conclusive action before they leave the booth.

Chapter 8 – Designing Your Booth

How are you going to attract potential customers to your booth? This is a multi-faceted question. Let's start with your booth design. Are you designing it in-house or using an outside vendor? That usually depends on the size of your company and your budget. If you have a limited budget, be aware of outside design companies because their job is to upsell. You might be better off with a little-less professional booth, but then be able to do more pre-market advertising or deeper promotions.

What size booth will you have? The size of your booth is the first impression that the attendee will have of you. Remember small or partial booths get little attention. Better to have a larger, less expensive booth than a smaller booth but you've spent a ton of money on.

Especially in distributor shows, I see row after row of rep booths that have 2' or less for each manufacturer's product displayed, all in a long line. Now, this may be fine if it is an ongoing line with no real market promotions and they're just there because they have to be.

Or if it's a vendor who has been there forever and dealers are just taking advantage of a market discount, that's fine, I guess. To me, that's just a status quo situation at best.

But if you're trying to build the business, introduce new products or add your program to new dealers or distributors, I really don't think this is an effective way to get it accomplished. With a half booth, at least you have the ability to showcase some new items as well as display the normal offering. Dealers have little perception of what could be, and your job is to show them the reality.

A 10'x10' booth gives you the ability to not only display your line but also have something to grab their attention like a banner, as well as a place to sit down to write an order. A well done 10'x20' booth shows you are a real player and deserves their attention as well as their business.

Again, *"Perception is Reality"* and I have often seen small factories place huge programs with both distributors and dealers because they presented themselves as serious companies rather than just startups. Also, if you look like you're well established, dealers will have more confidence in working with you. If you're already established and have the funds to have a large island booth, you know the importance of a large booth.

After deciding how big a booth you will go with, and what you're trying to accomplish, the next decision is how it will be laid out.

A big mistake many manufacturers make is focusing on selling their name. The back of their booth is filled with the company name XYZ or whatever. Unless you're Coca-Cola or some other household name, what is that going to get you? You're not selling your name or your company, but your product, so that message must be clear. I always ask the question WHY. Why should anyone have an interest in your booth, your product or in speaking to you?

Put yourself in the dealer's position, walking down aisle after aisle, booth after booth. Your ability to make a great first impression is paramount. First of all, most tend to look straight ahead as they don't want the hawkers to grab them when they have no interest. And grabbing dealers off the aisle usually just doesn't work. It generally just turns them off.

Having your promotion or new product visible up front with signage where it might attract their attention is vital.

I personally am not fond of backdrops that depict a plan-o-gram or display. It is appropriate for products like shelves of wire because everyone knows what a coil of wire is, but say, a display of connectors or tools, no way. Dealers still like to touch and feel.

Generally, I don't block the front of my booth with an 8' or 10' table, thereby blocking attendees from entering my booth. It's important to let dealers in to touch and feel. I always brought inexpensive 6' Lifetime adjustable tables and draped them myself. This offers much better access to your booth. Or I run that 8' table that is often provided, alongside the booth instead of in front. It gives you lots of access while keeping all of the tablespace.

I often place the chairs provided, up front, as a way for dealers to sit down and write orders but bring high stools if the booth personnel must sit down. This almost looks like your standing, ready to talk to them. If you bring the chairs into the booth, booth personnel will sit down and then get on their phones or computer rather than sell a product. Most dealers will walk right past a booth where the sales associates are sitting.

Another suggestion is to make sure your boot is lit. If you have a Pop-up display, buy the light kit. If you use gondolas, get an extra shelf, install it at the very top and attach a 4' single 5000K LED fixture underneath it. It attracts much more attention as the dealers walk down the aisle. Picture a long row of normal booths, then yours that is well lit up, that alone will grab their attention, if only for a moment. Just make sure you contract for electricity before the show.

Designing the actual layout.
Who will be designing your booth? If it's your in-house team, please make sure they understand your goals and what it takes to draw attendees into your booth. Way too often, Marketing gets hung up on some abstract cute idea and forget what the core goal is.

Let's talk image concept. You want to be so flagrant in your design that at only a moments glance, you will convey what you want them to know. That's because most of the time, that's all you get. The attendee is walking down your aisle, probably only once, is distracted by whom they're walking with and by exhibitors on both sides. Their mind also may be on the last conversation they just had or that disturbing phone call.

Very, very seldom do I find attendees slowly going down every aisle, checking each booth to see what might be of interest. Keeping that in mind that you only have that quick glance to attract them, should be vital in your design.

Designing a workable, inviting booth.
After deciding how big a booth you will go with, and what you're trying to accomplish, the next decision is how it will be laid out. In designing your booth layout, the first question is: what function are you planning to do in it?

Are you planning on sitting down and presenting a program based off of written material or a display screen? Then you probably need a small counter in front to start your initial conversation and a table or desk with chairs to go into detail and hopefully close the deal. Your backdrop must convey what you are offering and WHY they should be interested. This should be an open and uncluttered booth.

Maybe you're demonstrating a product and how it works; then obviously you need a demonstration table at the front edge of your booth and as well as room behind it so as to answer questions and take orders. Surprisingly a lot of demonstration booths do a great job in laying out the demonstration area and a poor job of providing a place to close the deal. Many on the attendee to take literature, hoping that they follow-up and order the product later. But most of that literature ends up in the trash sooner or later and the opportunity is wasted.

If you're going to demonstrate a product, have enough booth personnel to either take the order or their information, so the interest can be followed up on. Optimally, you should be able to contact every attendee that watched the demonstration so that you can close the deal.

If your only purpose for exhibiting is to thank existing customers, then your backdrop only needs your company name and maybe your slogan. Of course, you're going to rent comfortable furniture for your customers to sit on while you relay your appreciation for the business, but I prefer individual chairs rather than sofas. Unless it's a couple, most people are not comfortable sitting really close, side by side and you want them to feel relaxed. If possible, you should have two seating groups so that more than one customer group can be engaged at a time. This is one of the rare instances where corporate executives should be in the booth. You want the customer to know they are appreciated from management as well their normal sales contacts.

Another potential layout is in a *"Show only environment",* where you are just reminding customers what you have or are introducing new products, but not taking orders. This usually is with very mature companies with National or International presence. You are basically just reinforcing your market position. In this situation, you are emphasizing your name and products, maybe from different categories, that are displayed prominently around your booth. In this case, you want to make sure that the booth personnel are knowledgeable enough to explain what all of the different aspects of your organization are, so you get full exposure.

Lastly, the most prominent booth layout is where you are trying to get the attendee to start buying your product, whether directly or through a dealer/distributor. I have to admit that this is where most of my experience is, actually having product to show and either taking orders right there or getting the customer involved in a program. This is a very result oriented and quantifiable booth investment.

These layouts can vary but normally you have either a backdrop touting the type of product/category or a display of product, often a Plan-o-gram. Are you providing chairs for your attendees to sit down on? Shows are long & tiring. Though I'm careful not to block the booth with a table across the front, when it's necessary, I make sure that if they have interest and would like to talk (or place an order), they have the ability to that.

Regardless of your type of layout, having your promotion or new product visible up front with signage where it might attract their attention is vital.

Chapter 9 – Destination Booths

Is your Booth a Destination? Are they walking directly to your booth or are you on their list of *Must Sees*? If not, the probability of that potential customer paying attention to you as they walk down the aisle of a show with anywhere from 100 to 1000 booths or more is nil at best. Be a destination!!!!!!!

Can you answer these reasons WHY?
- Does the attendee know why are you exhibiting? What are your goals for them?
- Why will anyone know you are going to be there? What have you done to let potential customers know you are showing?
- Why will they come to your booth? Have you given them a solid reason to find you?
- Why should they buy your product? Quality, Price, Uniqueness, Service?
- Why should they buy right there? Important to close the deal while they're in front of you.
- Why should they remember you? Have you made yourself memorable?

All of these questions should already be answered in the attendee's mind before they ever get to the show. Most of them have already decided whom they will see, in what order they will see them and what they will do there.

Buying Shows

In a buying show, probably 80 to 90 % of all buying decisions are made before the market even starts. A prudent attendee has gone through the show book and made a list of who they need to see. You need to make sure that every attendee knows what you will be offering and WHY they should either stop by your booth to place an order or at least find out more about your program.

Depending on the type of show, there usually are several different ways to become a destination. Often the show has a way of sending out a pre-show mailer. If available, this is a perfect way to bring attention to what you are offering.

If you have been able to build or can borrow from a fellow exhibitor, a Data Base of attendees, then a well-constructed Pre-Market email campaign is perfect. But it can't be a one-shot attempt. First of all, it has to be simple and to the point, explaining what you're offering, why it's a good deal, show pictures, let them know what your booth number is and how they can contact you before the show. Try to make it attractive enough it will catch their attention.

If making appointments is appropriate, information on how to do that should be included. But this should be sent out at least twice. Once three weeks ahead of the show and again one week before the show. Make sure you include a link showing how they can eliminate additional emails from you.

I personally haven't found that paying for ads in show directories are worth the money. As an attendee, I never went through the show guide and found someone I wanted to go visit off of an ad.

If you're a very successful vendor with a lot of extra money, the overhead signs that hang from the ceiling to show attendees how to find you can be helpful. But I don't know that they bring new ones to your booth. The same thing can be accomplished almost as well by mounting those vertical banners on top of the backdrop posts and for one heck of a lot less money.

Non-Buying Shows
A non-buying show, again many attendees have already made plans about which key exhibitors they need to see.

Sometimes these can be the most difficult to become a destination for. Usually, these have a lot more attendees so pre-show emails or mailers can be very expensive and difficult to do.

Here is where advertising in whatever is available through the show's own opportunities may be worthwhile. Just make sure you are touting why they will be interested in your product or service, not just pushing your brand or company name. Again, include your booth number and contact information.

General ideas that draw in attendees
Please remember this one important saying *"Be Backs, Won't."* You usually get one shot at grabbing their attention.

Something I see utilized very little, but I really like, are those one-time, stick to the floor signs that you put right in front of your booth. They can be purchased inexpensively at Staples or Office Depot/Office Max. They really differentiate your booth from others, while people are walking down the aisle. Just make sure that the Convention Center allows it.

I am against the use of Celebrities for drawing attendees to your booth. I don't care whether it's an Athletic Star, a Racing Star, a Movie Star or Miss Whatever. YES, they will bring lots of people to your booth, a whole lot; but what are you gaining? Ask almost any individual walking away with an autographed poster what that booth sold or even what company it was, and very seldom will they have any idea. But they got their poster. The worst part is I've never seen an exhibitor have the necessary personnel there to grab the potential buyer with their new poster in hand and then lead them in to sell them something. Besides that, their booth is so crowded that truly interested attendees will just walk right on by.

Depending on the type of show, different incentives may be very successful.

Not that you might duplicate these, but here are some of the things I have used in the past. They might give ideas that will work for you.

When I had a couple of Tractor Dealerships, we were exhibiting in a Landscape Show where a lot of Japanese Growers were attending. These were our target customers in this area, and we needed to attract their attention. Now, don't take offense to the concept because, at this time, the use of furs was not frowned upon. Anyway, knowing these growers all brought their wives, we offered them a free fur jacket or coat depending on the number of tractors they bought. We had gotten them at no charge from a furrier in LA and only paid for what we gave away. It was a VERY successful show.

While running the sales for a major tool company, we were introducing the new Pack-in-Roll at the time. Knowing that at the time, Ace Hardware shows didn't provide carts for the dealers to tote their literature or personal things in, we decided to offer a free Pack-in-Roll with a minimum order. Then we would upsell them to other things as well. Well, the first show was too successful. We had brought in a few pallets of PNR, thinking that when dealers came in, we would unwrap the PNR, put a *"Got Mine Free at Booth 933"* label on them and then sell the heck out of the other products. Of course, we advertised this before the show. Within 15 minutes of opening, we had a line all of the way down the aisle of dealers wanting to place their $500 order and get their free PNR. This went on until we ran out of PNR. We were so busy unwrapping, putting labels on and running to get more, that we never had a chance to upsell. At the next show, we had them already unwrapped, labeled and had plenty of people in the booth to upsell. Still today, 17 years later, I occasionally see a PNR with our label still on it rolling down show aisles.

Then there was one of my vendors who had a really good idea of offering a Five Dollar bill to every dealer who came by their booth. They figured that it cost them more than that to get an interested dealer to stop by. It worked great until I found out that the vendor's employee was just handing out the Five Dollars without trying to sell anything. Great idea, poor execution.

At a distributor market only a few years ago, I had twenty-two vendors exhibiting in this two-day show. At this particular show, you could have all of your vendors together in one area. I had two goals: to introduce a new category of Houseware vendors and to dramatically build up my database of attending dealers. We asked each vendor to donate $100 each. For each vendor purchase, the dealer received a raffle ticket and then at the end of each day, we drew out one ticket. That dealer each day won $1000. The distributor salesman for those two dealers also won $100 each. It was a very successful promotion and still use that dealer database today.

Sometimes you can turn an exposure only show into a buying show with the right promotion. For years we exhibited in the Irrigation show which is strictly meant to be a place to meet your customers, introduce some new products for the season and be able to train the dealers/installers as to your product. But we wanted to make the booth pay for itself right then, so we let all of our distributors know that if they turned in their pre-season orders in there at the show, they would receive an extra discount, not only for the show order but for the whole season. This promotion insured we were their source for that entire year. VERY successful.

Some gimmicks are just not well thought out though. I was at a recent show where a vendor brought in a real, live caged Tiger. While some people walked by to see a live Tiger, most attendees thought it improper to bring a caged animal into a show and shied away.

But a popular Dog Food manufacturer brings his British Labs into the show and periodically has them do fetching tricks. During their off time, they lay around on elevated beds, enjoying the attention and petting from attendees. This is always a successful booth and the dogs seem to enjoy it as well.

Be careful of bringing in fancy Cars, Motorcycles or other toys. Make sure they have something to do with what you are selling, otherwise it could just be considered showing off. Again, while it may attract attention, is it distracting from the goal of your booth and using up valuable booth space. I have seen this work well, but also backfire.

Using giveaways as a memory tool is not a good way to get attendees to stop by. Candy, pens or such, just sitting on the table means nothing and they won't be useful after they walk away. Many exhibitors feel it's necessary to have something up front for the attendees to take with them, but are they a draw or a distraction? While a bowl of candy is nice for people to pick-up, doesn't it really distract their attention from looking at your booth? Can you really start to engage them just because they reached into your candy bowl?

Have you ever picked up a pen or gadget at a show, taken it back to your office, and then looked at it and said, *"I better give them a call?"* Probably not. Why not spend those marketing dollars on an award for them taking the time to talk to you, something that will make them remember you? An example might be a Note Book with your name & logo on the front. Sure, everyone puts everything on their phone or computer, but most people still write things down. Maybe it's a useable sample of what you're selling.

How about offering to give $1.00 for a worthwhile charity for stopping by your booth and listening to your pitch.

Using a monitor to showcase explicit product features and benefits is good, but just to show off your company is not. When they were new, I was a fan of monitors, but now they usually are a distraction. Often, they are just feeding the companies ego: Look at us and how important we are. Does the customer really care what your facility looks like or who your president is? NO, they want to know how you're going to solve their problem, their end-user's problem or just make them more money.

Chapter 10 – Booth Staff

Booth Personnel. Here is where I will make a lot of people uncomfortable. A booth should be manned by knowledgeable associates that know how to sell, not the most expendable person in the organization or someone you hire just to sit in a booth. This is WRONG; you just wasted all of the money spent being there and will get no results. Booth personnel should be knowledgeable, personable and have the ability to sell.

Please leave the Corporate Rock Star at home. You know who I'm talking about. They'll show up an hour into the show, rearrange the booth for no reason except to show their authority, piss off those who worked hard to set it up, then go off to talk to their old friends from the industry, never to be seen again until they leave for that golf game at home. Instead, spend that same amount of money on two knowledgeable associates who will stay in the booth and sell something.

Having inefficient, unqualified or unmotivated booth personnel is probably the biggest mistake most vendors make. I'll also add, expecting your rep to be able to sell your product as well as you can, especially if they have 43 lines is foolish. When you're able to actually get an attendee interested and willing to stop by your booth, you have to be ready to not only talk to them but inform them as to why they should buy your product and then tactfully close the sale.

That means you have to:
- Be standing in your booth ready to do business, not sitting in a corner on your cell phone or laptop.
- Be completely knowledgeable about the product & program and be capable of quoting and making decisions. I'm talking about making those big decisions, like volume discounts or important lead-times. If you expect them to come back in a half hour or you have to get back to them next week, you probably lost the opportunity. Remember again, **"Be Backs, Won't."** Or by the time they get back to their store, they are already immersed in daily challenges and will probably not remember what they talked about. The enthusiasm may be gone.

- Have enough qualified booth personnel to handle the opportunities. Every 10' booth should have two people and a 20' booth should have at least three. Nothing is worse than having a great potential walk away because no one is available to talk to them.

If your company exhibits in several trade shows a year, it may be worthwhile to have a completely separate set of associates that just plan, setup and work your booths. Of course, they have to be well versed on your product/programs, but a Sales Manager attending would help facilitate that. Having a separate and completely responsible staff should eliminate mistakes in what was designed, ordered and how everything is set up because they do it over and over.

To plan from the beginning, then execute correctly takes concentrated attention and if trade shows are a side-responsibility, it may not be done correctly. Hopefully, the Trade Show team takes pride in doing it perfectly and then also have absolute accountability.

Chapter 11- Working the Booth

Look like you're ready to talk with customers. That means standing or as mentioned before, resting on stools. Nothing tells a potentially attracted customer that you're really not that interested in them than sitting in a corner on your Smart Phone or buried deep into a project on your computer. Either be more professional and do your work before or after the show or have enough people to cover your booth so you can leave and do what is necessary at a common table away from your booth. Every attendee will tell you that this is the biggest turnoff, period.

Remember that slogan *"Attitude is Everything?"* Well, it couldn't be more important than in working a trade show. Every booth worker needs to be on their A game: happy, awake, personable and acting like the most important thing in their life is taking care of that customer. Everyone one of you can visualize that booth where the staff are just standing around, gloomy looks on their face thinking they would rather be anywhere but here. Who wants to be approached by them?

Order forms – If this is an order writing show, it is imperative that you have well-thought out, easy and quick to use order forms. They should be appropriate for this show, designed so that products are quick to find and that can be filled out in a very timely fashion. Customers have little patience for booth workers who have to search through computer files or price books for standard show pricing. It just shows you weren't prepared. But you should also have resources available to be able to quote/writeup special orders. Buyers understand it might take a bit to work up a special order, but you may lose the sale if you have to get back to them after the show. Close the deal while the customer is interested right then.

Dress codes – You should know what type of dress is required for your particular show. Some still do require Suits & Tie (Professional Attire for the ladies) and for others that may not be required but is appropriate. Others say Business Casual. Myself, I always tend to dress just on the higher end, a cut above what others do. Long Sleeve business shirts with the company logo are perfect in most situations.

Please do not require the ladies working your booth to wear men's shirts that not only look like they don't fit right but also make them feel uncomfortable. Pay as much attention to making them look good as you do the men. <u>They will probably outsell the men anyway.</u>

Sexy clothes may seem like a good idea, but they're not unless you're at an Automotive show or something like that. The general audience usually won't appreciate it. Men may feel awkward or be there for the wrong reason and many women get offended. Just not professional.

Wear comfortable shoes. Shows are long and if you are in pain by noon, how attentive will you be. You will not lose a single order by not being in heels. And take it from someone with over a half-century of shows, all of that standing will really hurt you in the long run if you don't pay attention. I wish I had.

Always layer up. You never know what the temperature will be inside a convention center and usually, the hotter it is outside, the colder it will be inside. I wish I had a dollar for every vendor I saw freezing in their booth because they didn't plan ahead.

Unless it is a rural type show, regular jeans on men are just disrespectful. You're spending a lot of money on an image so why not look the best yourself. That goes for unkept shirts or shirts that fit 3 sizes ago. Look in the mirror and ask yourself, Am I the image I want to portray.

Be on time, ready to sell before the show opens. Already have your coffee if necessary but beware of coffee or cigarette breath. Nothing will turn a potential buyer off more than being approached by someone with Goat Breath.

This should be obvious but don't eat in your booth. If you're like me, I need something every couple of hours, so I make sure it's a simple protein bar I can nibble unobtrusively on in-between customers. But sitting down with a plate of food in your booth while trying to take care of customers is just not proper.

Are you completely prepared with the proper literature, pricing information, lead retention sheets, business cards etc.? Excellent

Handout Literature is critical. It has to be relevant to what you are promoting at this show. It must list the promotions, the reasons they should buy from you, the costs and have the info to contact you. Just standard factory literature means nothing and only you get excited that you have a million square feet of warehouse. They just want to know how you will make them more money. The literature has to be self-explanatory enough that it will sell their bosses when they get back to the office. They should be on heavy glossy stock, full color and printed on both sides. This will help your literature stand out from all of the other paper in their bag when they get home. I often have used a fancy paper clip to hold all of a vendors' literature together, so it doesn't get lost in the stack.

I use Catalog Kings and I've found them to be the absolute most reasonable printer and VERY affordable. Their contact info is Gregg Gache @ Catalog Kings, Direct Line: 800.515.3940, Greg Gache, Greg@catalogkings.com. Tell him Bert referred you for very special pricing.

Please be early and alert so you're all set to take care of them even before the attendees get there.

You're there to sell, not party. This isn't an excuse to let loose, just because you're away from home. You or your company has spent a lot of money to gain additional business, why waste it because you think your still Eighteen.

Pre-design your opening lines and practice them. Make them inviting and creative. Don't use stupid stuff like. "Can I show you something." Or "How are you today?" "Do you know about our product?" Put yourself in their shoes, walking down the aisle getting hounded by booth after booth. Design an opening line like "Hi. Our product safely eliminates mold far better than any other. May I show you how?"

Keep your booth clean and free of clutter. Store your gear out of sight. A well-designed booth image is ruined by backpacks laying all over.

If you're a rep, either have business cards with each manufacturers name on them or have space on your card to write the vendors name on it AND do it. Why hand out a card that is ambiguous, so when they get back to their businesses, they have no idea who you were with.

For factory people, don't hand out generic company cards. Most companies have automated phone systems which mean it is very difficult to get who you want without all of their information. Each booth worker who expects to be contacted should their own specific business cards.

Though it's becoming more difficult, try to schedule meetings with current or potential customers, then make sure you're available at that time to sit down with them and give them your complete attention. Obviously, you need enough booth personnel to cover the booth while you're in your meeting.

One of the hardest things I've struggled to overcome is when you're talking to a minor potential or existing customer and the Mr./MS Big Wig shows up and looks interested. You hate to lose the super opportunity but don't want to be rude either. Everyone is important, but some are just critical to your success. The only solution I've found is to let them know you had an appointment with this other customer and hand them tactfully over to another booth personnel.

If you exhibit in reoccurring markets and you may see the same attendees over and over again, you not only have to remember their names but their companies and what their interest in your product is. Now that may be easy for some people, but my mind doesn't work that way, so I have to find ways to cheat on it. I find that if I have time, I will write down notes on the conversation trying to cover as much as I quickly can. Then I will try and review this before each day of the show.

It also really helps if the show's badges have the names large enough that you can read as their walking up. Then you can use their first name as part of your opening line, especially if you've talked to them before. It also helps if the town where they're from is on the badge. Then, unless it's from a large town, somewhere during the conversation, you can ask what's that near.

Towards the beginning of the conversation, I always ask who their customer base is. That's critical to how you structure your sales pitch. Way too many salespeople immediately start selling their product without first finding out how it will help the person talking to. Your ability to focus directly to their needs will keep them interested rather than turning them off because it doesn't relate to them.

Seems like selling today has become a lost art. Learn all you can about how to do it right and pay attention to those that do. I'm not talking about hard-core, pushing customers into a corner, so they have to buy, but selling to their needs. Ask questions first, find out if your product or service an actually help them then explain how your product can do that. Finally, *"Ask for the Order."* I'm utterly shocked how few sales people do that today.

Chapter 12 - Post-market Follow-up

One of the most important goals of any Trade Show is to build a Data Base of Potential/Existing/Past customers. This is the best way to develop a comprehensive way of contacting customers about whatever it is you are trying to accomplish before each show and other promotions during the year. There are many ways of doing this:

- Some organizations will share their attendee listing, but if they do, it may be expensive and too inclusive. Use it only if the list is affordable and it's sortable. You need a Data Base of potential clients only.
- If the show has a badge scanning program, use it, for every person that stops by.
- Offer some incentive to leave their business card and make sure it had their email address on it. Get creative. After you have compiled that listing, make sure it is put into a specific Trade Show Contact Data Base and use it right away. Make sure that it is easily sortable, so you can use it in different ways. Now you have a way to let potential/existing customers remember what you did offer, know what you will be offering at the next market, plus contact them between shows with reasons to do business with you. Use it consistently but

not so often that it loses its significance! Always make sure you include a way for them to opt-out of your list if they want.

Chapter 13 – Maximizing Your Returns (A Summary)

- Have an effective Marketing Plan
- Initiate a realistic budget
- Choose the correct show
- Design an effective and appropriate booth
- Plan your promotions
- Print your literature
- Pre-Show Advertising making your booth a destination
- Coordinate shipping on a timely basis
- Decide who will man the booth and train them
- Work the show
- Process the orders as soon as possible.
- Follow-up with all leads after the show until each lead is closed or dead.
- Do an honest critique of all aspects of the show and note all changes that you need to make for the next one.

Hopefully, this Guide will increase your Trade Show Success. Shouldn't everyone that's involved with your shows have one?

This is a working guide and will be updated as appropriate. If you have additional ideas, stories or suggestions, please send them to:
Bert Kenyon – **Bert@BertKenyon.com**
They will be added to the next addition.

If this guide has shown you that I have enough experience to personally help your program and would like one on one help, please contact me. I have several different options that should meet most companies needs and budgets.
Bert Kenyon – **Bert@BertKenyon.com**
www.BertKenyon.com

www.ingramcontent.com/pod-product-compliance
Lightning Source LLC
Chambersburg PA
CBHW030019190526
45157CB00016B/3134